Charles Darwin

Visionary Behind
The Theory of Evolution

Anna Sproule

BLACKBIRCH™
PRESS

THOMSON

GALE

Detroit • New York • San Diego • San Francisco • Cleveland
New Haven, Conn. • Waterville, Maine • London • Munich

THOMSON

GALE

For more information, contact
The Gale Group, Inc.
27500 Drake Rd.
Farmington Hills, MI 48331-3535
Or you can visit our Internet site at http://www.gale.com

LIBRARY OF CONGRESS CATALOGING-IN-PUBLICATION DATA

Sproule, Anna.
  Charles Darwin / by Anna Sproule.
    p. cm. — (Giants of science)
Includes bibliographical references (p. 63).
  ISBN 1-56711-655-8 (hardback : alk. paper)
  1. Darwin, Charles, 1809-1882—Juvenile literature. 2.
Naturalists—England—Biography—Juvenile literature. [1. Darwin,
Charles, 1809-1882. 2. Naturalists. 3. Evolution.] I. Title. II.
Series.
  QH31.D2 .S74 2003
  576.8'092—dc21
                                            2002003240

Contents

Introduction: Too Late

Charles Darwin was too late. His life's work had been wasted. The exploration of the black land and its mysteries, the years of research, the endless sifting of fact after fact now seemed to count for nothing.

It had been twenty-three years since Darwin, naturalist and future country gentleman, had started his great hunt for the truth. And he was sure he had found it. If only he had managed to finish the book he was writing! If only he had been less painstaking, less anxious to address every possible argument or objection—but it was too late to do things differently now.

A rival had arrived at the truth as well: a rival who would soon tell the world what he had discovered. A rival who had, ironically, come to Darwin for friendship and help.

As Darwin, stooped and grim-faced, plodded on his midday walk, he knew he was facing the greatest crisis of his life.

In the Galápagos Islands, a marine iguana (opposite) surveys its rock-lined habitat, while a giant tortoise (below) paces through the island scrub.

The Black Land

Sweet and fresh, the scents of early summer drifted past him. But he paid them no attention. In his mind, he was far from the English countryside and years away from the present year of 1858.

He was back in a place where the Pacific Ocean's waves broke endlessly on a scorching black beach. On black rocks too hot for a man to touch, big dark lizards sprawled luxuriously. Monstrous tortoises ambled by, munching cactus. Above them, perched on the cactus spines, small birds twittered. Over everything hung a harsh, heavy smell, as if the dry scrub were on fire.

Darwin thought back to this land where, in 1835, his work had all begun: the Galápagos Islands. In Spanish, he remembered, they were also called the Enchanted Isles—although while he was there

someone had remarked that the place looked like hell itself. So, in that sense at least, Darwin thought grimly, hell was where his current problems had all started.

A Shocking Letter

The Enchanted Isles and their black rocks faded from Darwin's mind. Into their place came other, newer memories: the drawing room a few hours ago, and the little heap of letters waiting for him. Among them was one from the East Indies. It had been sent by Darwin's fellow naturalist, Alfred Russel Wallace.

Wallace's letter had felt heavy. Cheerfully, Darwin had ripped it open, pulled out the thick sheaf of pages it contained, and sat down to read them. As he read, his contented mood vanished. Far away in the Moluccas, however, Wallace sounded cheerful enough for two. He had recently recovered from malaria. While he was sweating and shivering in the grip of the illness, he had had the most amazing idea: a flash of inspiration. He had worked out how different kinds of living things, or species, were created.

The Struggle to Survive

All living things, Wallace recognized, faced a continuous struggle for survival. They were preyed upon; they fell ill; they starved. Dangers threatened all species and, sometimes, all the members of a single species. Why then, did some creatures die, and others live?

The answer, Wallace believed, lay in the small differences that occurred between organisms that were otherwise similar. For example, the fastest animals in a group could outrun their enemies. The most intelligent could outwit them. And the healthiest—the strongest and best fed—could shake off diseases that killed weaker group members. Only the best equipped for survival stood much chance of living.

The best-equipped organisms had young with a better chance of survival too. They might well

"Let us take the case of a wolf, which preys on various animals, securing some by craft, some by strength, and some by fleetness; and let us suppose that the fleetest prey, a deer for instance, had from any change in the country increased in numbers, or that other prey had decreased in numbers, during that season of the year when the wolf was hardest pressed for food. Under such circumstances the swiftest and slimmest wolves would have the best chance of surviving and so be preserved or selected."

Charles Darwin, from *The Origin of Species*

inherit their parents' unusual speed, cunning, or strength. And so might their children, and their children's children. Very slowly, new varieties of animals emerge: new types, in which all the animals share some special, extra quality that aids survival.

Wallace's letter—4,000 words of explanation and argument, written in a feverish frenzy of inspiration—outlined this theory. The cat's claws, the falcon's great talons, the long neck with which the giraffe reached high into trees for its food: Wallace's theory covered them all. Although the paper had been written quickly, it was ready for other scientists to read and assess; in fact, it was ready for publication. Wallace himself, however, had one question: Did Darwin think it was any good?

A Life's Work

Under the cool trees in his garden, Darwin realized he was sweating. Of course he thought Wallace's work was good. It was admirable. He understood it

. . . .

"Those that prolong their existence can only be the most perfect in health and vigour; . . . the weakest and least perfectly organized must always succumb."

Alfred Russel Wallace, from the paper read to the Linnean Society in 1858

. . . .

For much of his life, Darwin lived and worked in this house that he shared with his wife and children.

as well as if he had written it himself. Every idea, every link in the argument: he knew them all like old friends. In fact, he had been living with them for years—beginning with his arrival in the Enchanted Isles and his observations of the region's strange inhabitants.

Wallace had had his great idea about the struggle for survival just a short while ago, in 1858. He, Darwin, had reached the same basic conclusions in the late 1830s—but only a few people knew that.

He had first mapped out his own species theory in 1842, and he had been working ever since to expand, confirm, and polish it. His friends kept urging him to make his ideas public, to write a book, and, two years ago, he had begun to do so. It was going to be a big

This portrait of Charles Darwin depicts him in 1840 at the age of thirty-one.

book. It had to be, to include all the facts he had collected to support his hypothesis of "natural selection"—the way in which nature itself works to bring new species into existence.

The book represented his life's work. He had wanted it to be perfect. Now, however, the scientific world seemed to be working just like the natural one. Success would go to the swiftest, to the first to publish—to Wallace, not Darwin.

A Matter of Trust

What made the situation worse was that Wallace had come to Darwin for assistance. Wallace trusted him to send the paper on to another scientist, the influential geologist Sir Charles Lyell. How could Darwin let his

> "I happened to read for amusement Malthus on 'Population', and being well prepared to appreciate the struggle for existence which everywhere goes on from long-continued observation of the habits of animals and plants, it at once struck me that under these circumstances favourable variations would tend to be preserved, and unfavourable ones to be destroyed. The result of this would be the formation of new species."
>
> **Charles Darwin**

fellow naturalist down? If he did, he would be guilty of the worst form of double-dealing—he would be betraying a trust to further his own ends.

Darwin knew he must send the manuscript to Sir Charles at once, today. It was the right thing to do—the only thing. And, after that, Darwin himself would not be able to publish his own views. His life's work would soon become a footnote to someone else's published ideas. He was not sure he could bear that.

Unaware of where he had been going, Darwin found himself back at the house. Wearily, he pushed open the tall glass door, and made his way inside.

The Book that Changed the World

Darwin never finished his "big book," but neither was he forced to give up his life's work, and the renown that deservedly accompanied it. His conscience would have allowed him to let Wallace take all the credit for the species theory, but Lyell and Darwin's other friends had a better idea. They arranged for his own early sketch to be presented, together with Wallace's paper, at a meeting of top-level British scientists.

Darwin and his supporters all realized that there was no time to lose. Wallace, they knew, might soon produce his own book. Darwin had to publicize his own findings on natural selection as quickly as possible. If he did not hurry, his chances would be finished for good.

Before the end of the summer, Darwin had started to write a much shorter, simpler version of his longer work. It took him nearly a year but this, for Darwin, was lightning-fast. On November 24, 1859, the book was published. *The Origin of Species* changed the world.

At first glance, Darwin's groundbreaking book did not seem so remarkable. It ranged over many aspects of biology, the science of living things. The first chapter, for example, looked at the breeding of domestic plants and animals such as roses, strawberries, cows, and pigeons. Other chapters looked at animal instincts and at geology and fossils.

These four species of Galápagos finches all have different types of beaks. Differences like these helped Darwin develop his theory of evolution.

The third and fourth chapters, however, were the ones that most revolutionized scientific thought. These chapters introduced the ideas at the heart of Darwin's thinking—the struggle for existence in the wild, the survival of the best equipped, and the whole process of natural selection that leads to the evolution of new species.

Many religions are founded on the idea of a divine designer. Above, a deity of the ancient Greeks, the harvest goddess Demeter, sends a charioteer to earth with instructions on how to plant her great gift of corn.

"In His Own Image"

Today, Darwin's theory of evolution is well known and widely accepted by most scientists and nonscientists alike. In Darwin's own day, however, the theory was novel and shocking. It contradicted ideas and beliefs that had been accepted as truth for hundreds, if not thousands, of years.

In the nineteenth century, the world—and world thought—was dominated by the Christian nations of the West. And most Christians believed that all creatures and plants were literally the work of God. They had been shaped once, and for all time, by a divine designer in the days after he first created the world

itself. Many Christians were also quite sure about the date of the world's creation. Two clergymen had calculated that God had made the world on October 23, 4004 B.C.

Most importantly, all believers knew that, in God's scheme of things, human beings played a special role. Like other creatures, they, too, were the work of God. Unlike any other living thing, however, they shared something of God's own power and glory—because, according to the Bible, God had shaped them "in his own image."

A Formula for Revolution

Darwin's book challenged these ideas. It removed God—a benevolent, caring God—from the picture. It also challenged the idea of purposeful, permanent design. Instead, it said that living things were constantly changing, evolving, and being reshaped by the random forces of nature. Most shocking of all, at the very end of his book, Darwin had even included a hint that humans—far from being special—were as subject to the laws of natural selection as any other living things.

To most Christian believers everywhere, the implications of Darwin's great theory were world-shattering. If Darwin was correct, their own views on the universe and their place in it simply fell apart. Therefore, when *The Origin of Species* was first published, it caused a hurricane of furious—and terrified—protest.

Soon, however, scientists began to agree with Darwin's theories. Other people followed suit and, even before Darwin died, the ideas that had once seemed so dangerous had largely become part of the nineteenth-century European worldview.

The Origin of Species was not simply a book about biology. It was a formula for revolution. And its painstaking, perfectionist author was one of the world's great revolutionaries.

Opposite: This painting, by sixteenth-century artist Raphael, depicts the Christian God creating the world.

• •

"The 'Darwinian Revolution' has always ranked alongside the 'Copernican Revolution' as one of those episodes in which a new scientific theory symbolizes a wholesale change in cultural values."

Peter J. Bowler, from *Evolution: The History of an Idea*

• •

This painting shows Charles Darwin as a boy, with his younger sister Catherine.

"A Disgrace to Yourself"

Charles Darwin was born on February 12, 1809, the fifth child and second son of Robert Darwin, a successful and highly respected doctor, and his wife, Susannah, a member of the well-known family of Wedgwood pottery manufacturers. Charles grew up in the prosperous country town of Shrewsbury, amid a landscape full of gardens and hedges, bordered by a great river. School, in which he was taught mostly Latin and Greek, bored him. Whenever he could escape from it, he spent time rambling through the woods. He loved to collect things like rocks and insects. He also loved dogs, plants, fishing, and his father, Robert—a mountain of a man who inspired awe in all who met him, including his children.

Robert, however, was disappointed in his son, and once told him, in a fit of despair, "You care for

nothing but shooting, dogs, and rat-catching, and you will be a disgrace to yourself and all your family." Darwin's teachers shared his father's opinion. In fact, in his youth, no one thought young Charles would ever amount to much.

The Search for a Profession

The Darwin family's prosperity ensured that Charles would never be short of money when he grew up. Still, he was the son of a professional man, and as he grew older, people thought he ought to enter some profession himself. The question was, which one?

Robert Darwin decided that his son might make a good physician. Medicine seemed a logical choice. Not only was the senior Darwin a doctor, but Charles's elder brother, Erasmus, was already studying the subject at Edinburgh University. So, at the age of sixteen, Charles set out for Edinburgh.

Life there, he found, offered Charles plenty of opportunities for doing the things he liked best. He collected sea creatures. He met other people who were interested in biology. He joined a natural history society; he wrote up his seashore findings and read aloud to his new friends what he had written.

· ·

"I tried to make out the names of plants, and collected all sorts of things, shells, seals, franks, coins, and minerals. The passion for collecting which leads a man to be a systematic naturalist, a virtuoso, or a miser, was very strong in me, and was clearly innate."

Charles Darwin, describing himself at the age of eight

· ·

Darwin was born in Shrewsbury, England, in 1800, in a house overlooking the River Severn.

Charles, however, hated medicine. He found the lectures even duller than his Latin classes had been. Anatomy disgusted him; hospital work filled him with horror. Worst of all were the operations. In those days before anesthetics, surgery was a nightmare of screams, blood, and agony. Darwin attended two of these dreadful sessions in the operating room. He never went a third time.

Life at Cambridge

When it became apparent that Darwin would not succeed in medicine, his family suggested he try the clergy instead. Good-naturedly, he agreed—the life of a country clergyman sounded pleasant enough. Churchmen were required to have degrees, so he attended Cambridge University, and plunged with gusto into a different sort of student life.

With his friends—a boisterous, hard-drinking group—he wined, dined, and played cards late into the night. By day, he attended to his two ruling passions, collecting beetles and shooting. He worked endlessly in his dorm room to improve his aim, firing blanks at a candle held by a courageous friend. If the candle went out, he knew his aim had been accurate.

The noise bewildered the professors. "What an extraordinary thing it is," one said. "Mr. Darwin seems to spend hours in cracking a horse-whip in his room, for I often hear the crack when I pass under the windows."

Other professors reacted differently to young Darwin. Two were so impressed by his scientific interests that they became his friends. One was John Henslow, a botanist. Henslow broadened Darwin's plant knowledge enormously. He took him on botany expeditions, welcomed him to his house, and urged him to read the books of the well-known German explorer and naturalist Alexander von Humboldt.

Though his days were busy, Darwin still managed to get his degree. In the summer of 1831, he went with another professor, the geologist Adam Sedgwick,

Darwin's mother was a member of the well-known family of Wedgwood pottery manufacturers. Top: The Wedgwood family medallion. Bottom: A piece of Wedgwood pottery.

on a trip to Wales to study rock formations and hunt for fossils. Then, on August 29, Darwin went home to Shrewsbury. There, he found waiting for him two letters that changed his life.

An Amazing Invitation

One of the letters came from Darwin's friend Henslow. The other was from another Cambridge scientist, George Peacock. Together, they contained an amazing invitation—a chance to go on a voyage around the world.

The British government, George Peacock's letter explained, was doing a survey of the South American coast and some of the Pacific islands. Peacock had been asked to recommend someone to act as the

This portrait shows the Wedgwood family at home on the family estate in Shropshire. Darwin's mother is on horseback in the middle of the painting, with her brother Josiah beside her.

voyage's naturalist: to observe, record, and collect anything of interest in the lands the ship visited. He had passed this request on to Henslow. Henslow's letter said that he had recommended Darwin for the job. The survey ship, HMS *Beagle*, would soon be leaving. Would Darwin be able to go with it?

Darwin could scarcely believe it. Why would the explorers want him, a mere beginner in the natural sciences? Henslow had the answer. The *Beagle's* captain was a young man, not much older than Darwin himself. He wanted the company of a friend and equal on the voyage. If the captain met Darwin and liked him, the search for a naturalist would be over.

A "Man of Common Sense"

Overwhelmed by his luck, Darwin was about to send his acceptance to Henslow. He had, however, momentarily forgotten about his father. For years, Dr. Darwin had been trying to steer his wayward son into a worthwhile career. The thought of his son traveling around the world on the *Beagle* did not please Dr. Darwin at all. He refused to give his approval—unless one condition was met. "If," he told Charles, "you can find any man of common sense who advises you to go I will give my consent."

All his life, Charles Darwin had been dominated by his father. Now, when everything hung on a strong will, he could not find it in himself to rebel. He did not even consider it. Sadly, the young man wrote to Henslow with his refusal. Then he set off to visit his Wedgwood relations. The partridge-hunting season was about to start, and he did not want to miss its opening days.

Darwin told his uncle, Josiah Wedgwood, about the offer he had received. And, to his joy, Uncle Jos reacted quite differently from his father. The *Beagle* trip, Uncle Jos said, was a splendid chance, a chance to be seized with both hands. He promptly dragged his nephew away from his shooting and, in a race against time, hurried him home.

· ·

"It is intolerable to think of spending one's whole life like a neuter bee living all one's days solitarily in smoky, dirty London. Only picture to yourself a nice soft wife on a sofa, with good fire and books and music perhaps. . . . Marry, Marry, Marry!"

Charles Darwin

· ·

Back in Shrewsbury, Dr. Darwin found himself faced both with his imploring son and his masterful brother-in-law. He had to admit that Josiah was a "man of common sense." He could not oppose Josiah's reasoning. He consented to Charles taking his round-the-world voyage.

Darwin's Nose

Darwin raced to London in hopes that the position had not yet been filled. He was in luck: the *Beagle's* captain, Robert FitzRoy, had offered the job to someone else, but that person had turned it down. On September 5, Darwin sat down for an interview with FitzRoy.

At first, FitzRoy didn't like him—because Darwin's nose was too small and snub! The captain had a theory that you could tell a man's character by his nose. FitzRoy's own nose was long, curved, and aristocratic, as befitted someone who descended from King Charles II. Darwin, he thought, had the nose of a weak man. Therefore, FitzRoy hesitated to hire him for a voyage of several years, around the world.

Darwin's enthusiasm and good nature, however, quickly won the captain over. Everything was settled, and the trip was on. It didn't matter that the ship's naturalist would not be paid for his work. Dr. Darwin would cover his son's expenses.

Instantly, the young man plunged into a frenzy of packing. He urged his family to send him his microscope and walking shoes. He ordered twelve new shirts and, on FitzRoy's advice, bought a rifle and pistols. Then he and the captain journeyed to Plymouth to see the *Beagle*.

Meeting the *Beagle*

Even by the standards of the time, the *Beagle* was small. More than seventy people were expected to live in this tiny craft while it followed its long route through the oceans of the world. Darwin, however, was impressed with the ship.

> "The voyage of the *Beagle* has been by far the most important event in my life, and has determined my whole career; yet it depended on so small a circumstance as my uncle offering to drive me thirty miles to Shrewsbury."
>
> Charles Darwin

Darwin used a microscope like this one in his research.

19

Before the *Beagle* set sail, Darwin became ill. The ship's departure had been delayed, and while he waited, Darwin noticed a rash had broken out on his hands. Aghast, he realized he had chest pains, too. Was there something wrong with his heart? He did not dare go to a doctor for fear he would be told he could not go on the voyage. The pains grew no worse, however, and at last, on December 27, 1831, the *Beagle* set off into the Atlantic Ocean for a five-year journey. Darwin was twenty-two years old.

Experiences of a Lifetime

After sixty-three days at sea, Darwin found himself standing in a grove in a lush tropical forest. Looking around, he felt delight flood through him. He had arrived in South America.

Darwin had always loved all aspects of the natural world: birds and animals, plants, and insects that fed on them. Now, he was in a paradise. All around him, creatures darted and fluttered. Exotic plants filled the air with unfamiliar perfumes.

The first tropical forest Darwin visited was near Salvador, in the Brazilian region of Bahia. From there, he journeyed on down the Brazilian coast to Rio de Janeiro, then on to Buenos Aires, Tierra del Fuego, and Cape Horn. As the *Beagle* came and went on her surveying tasks, Darwin was put ashore for days—even weeks—to do his own job of observing and collecting. And, at every stop, there were moments of supreme joy, excitement, and freedom.

The harshness of his travels seemed to toughen young Darwin's skin. During the journey, he became a man of action, strong and energetic.

In Montevideo, FitzRoy was asked to help put down a rebellion. Bristling with firearms, Darwin paraded the streets with the rest of the crew. While exploring on shore in Tierra del Fuego, FitzRoy and Darwin risked being stranded when a freak wave nearly washed their boat away. Darwin dashed

Top: This painting shows the Beagle *making port in Sydney, Australia, during its voyage around the world. Darwin's quarters were at the stern, under the flag.*

Left: *August Earle, the artist who accompanied the* Beagle, *created this painting that shows living conditions on a typical ship of Darwin's day.*

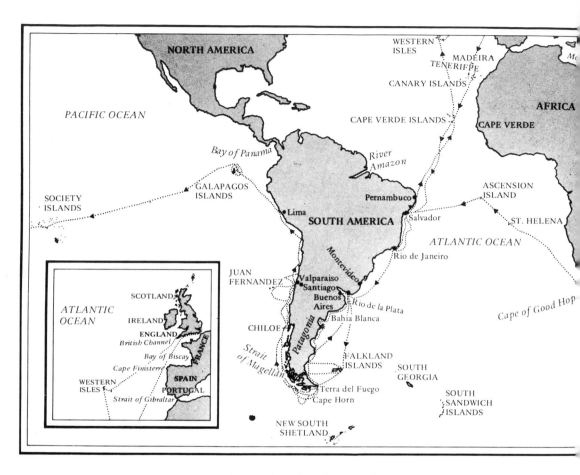

forward and grabbed it before it vanished. When the *Beagle* returned north again, doubling back on her tracks, Darwin spent weeks in a saddle; he rode across the Argentinian pampas, lived off the land, and slept under the stars.

Collecting Evidence

Darwin's skill with a rifle made him a useful member of any foraging party. But his main use for it was to shoot specimens that could be skinned, stuffed, and sent home to England. Photography had not yet been invented, so the best way to record a particular animal's appearance was to kill a specimen and preserve

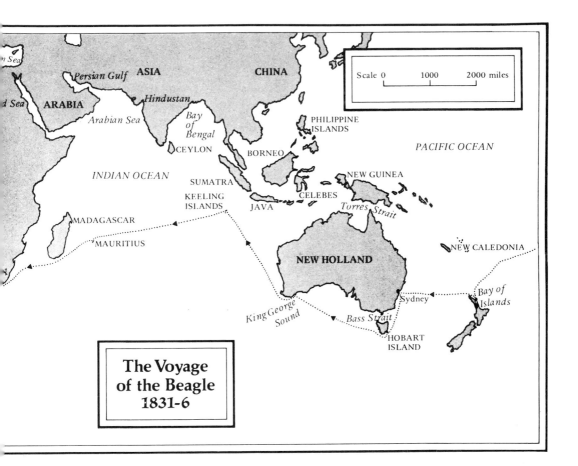

Scale 0   1000   2000 miles

PACIFIC OCEAN

ASIA

CHINA

ARABIA   Persian Gulf

Hindustan

Arabian Sea   Bay of Bengal

PHILIPPINE ISLANDS

CEYLON   BORNEO

INDIAN OCEAN   SUMATRA

NEW GUINEA

KEELING ISLANDS   CELEBES

JAVA   Torres Strait

MADAGASCAR   MAURITIUS

NEW CALEDONIA

NEW HOLLAND

Sydney   Bay of Islands

King George Sound   Bass Strait

HOBART ISLAND

The Voyage of the Beagle 1831-6

the body. Carefully, Darwin packed up box after box to send back to Henslow: stuffed mice, bags of seed, fish in pickling jars, and insects in nests of cotton wool.

These specimens did not always travel well— Henslow once complained that some of the mice were covered in fungus! No decay, however, could threaten one specific group of specimens that the ship's naturalist collected. They had once been living tissue, but now they were made of stone. They were the fossilized skeletons of creatures that, many thousands of years ago, had roamed across Argentina's vast plains.

This map shows the Beagle's route on its voyage of discovery.

The skeletons were enormous. Darwin had stumbled on a graveyard of the giants, what he called "a catacomb for monsters of extinct races."

The Giants' Graveyard

The giants' graveyard was a place called Punta Alta, close to the little Argentinian town of Bahía Blanca. The first bones Darwin unearthed had once belonged to a vast sloth-like creature called *Megatherium*. Like a modern sloth, this animal fed on leaves. It did not, however, have to climb through branches to get them. It was easily big enough to sit on its hindquarters, reach up into a tree, and tear the branches down.

The next fossil that Darwin found was another gigantic tree-browser, the *Megalonyx*. Then came a *Scelidotherium*, an animal that resembled both an anteater and an armadillo—and was the size of a rhinoceros. Darwin discovered several more remains of this type, and then some others that were truly baffling. One was a horse fossil. Darwin wondered

On his trip, Darwin came to know the herdsmen, or guasos, *of Chile. This painting depicts guasos and their wives.*

how a horse could have been in South America so long before the Spaniards were known to have brought the animals to the continent in the 1500s. Another find, the *Toxodon*, was a rodent the size of an elephant—a rodent that lived mainly in the water. The *Toxodon* was like an amazing cross between a rat and a hippo. It resembled a gigantic capybara, the modern world's largest rodent.

Filled with excitement, Darwin had his huge finds hauled back to the *Beagle*, where he stored them on the deck. The sailors jokingly moaned about the mess Darwin made of their tidy ship. Meanwhile, Darwin brooded intently over his precious finds. What was the link between the fossil creatures and their smaller modern equivalents? Why had these huge creatures died out? How had they died?

Seeds of Doubt

Devout Christians, Darwin knew, had an answer to these questions. According to the Bible, in ancient times, God had sent a great flood to punish the wicked world. During the flood, Noah had rescued members of most of the world's species by collecting them on his ark. These species, Christians believed, still continued to exist. But *Megatherium* and the rest had not been so lucky. Left outside the ark, they were overwhelmed by the floodwaters, and their species became extinct.

Darwin, as a former clerical student, knew what the Bible said. He was, however, beginning to doubt the flood theory. Other Christian teachings bothered him as well. Geologists were now theorizing that the earth was much, much older than Christian tradition maintained. The Church taught that the world's history only went back a few thousand years, while the scientists thought a few million years was a more accurate estimate.

Scientists also began to believe that the world's surface had been shaped slowly—rather than suddenly, in

Bones like these are one kind of fossil. Fossils are evidence of life in the distant past, preserved in stone.

floods sent by an angry God. Such things as volca-
noes, rivers, and oceans were the elements that
ceaselessly changed the face of the earth. And
changes were also taking place in the conditions in
which the earth's animals and plants lived. Climates
altered; places got hotter or colder, wetter or drier.

Perhaps, Darwin thought, some change in living
conditions had chased the giants out of existence.
But what could this change have been? Why should
all the animals have died? And how did their
smaller versions—the sloth and the armadillo,
for example—fit into the picture? In ancient times,
did these smaller animals encroach on the giants'
territory, and eat all their food?

Population Limits

Darwin was convinced that something had happened,
even if he was not sure yet what that something had
been. After all, there were limits on the population of
every species. Without such limits, the world would

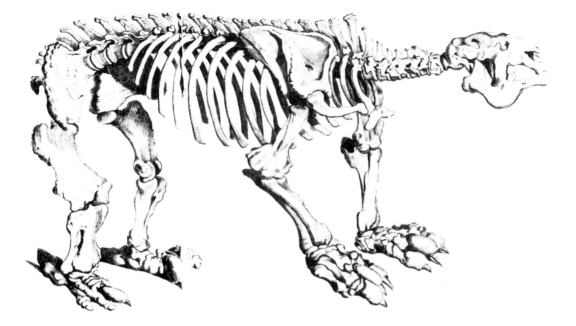

have been overrun and overgrown a million times over. Darwin was not sure just how this check on population growth worked. He was, however, absolutely certain it happened.

Darwin knew, too, the check could sometimes be overly effective. The numbers of a plant or animal species could start to free-fall, causing the species to become rarer and rarer. It was not difficult, Darwin reasoned, to predict the next stage. A rare species could easily become extinct. Was this what had happened to the monsters of the past? It was logical to think so. To Darwin, this concept made sense— more sense than the biblical stories of the great flood. He knew, however, that to challenge accepted beliefs would not be easy.

Forces of Nature

By the time the *Beagle* entered the Pacific Ocean, Darwin had abandoned his halfhearted plan to become a clergyman when he returned home. He

Opposite: This drawing from a supposedly scientific book of 1553 shows that the authors knew little about the actual appearance of extinct creatures.

Above: Darwin discovered the fossilized remains of the Megatherium, *a creature similar to a sloth, but much larger.*

Top and opposite bottom: The present-day equivalents of the fossilized giants Darwin discovered near Bahía Blanca: the two-toed sloth (above), the capybara (bottom right) and the armadillo (bottom far right). The sloth's prehistoric counterpart was the elephant-sized Megatherium.

now knew what he was going to do with his professional life. He would go on as he had begun—as a naturalist.

He voyaged up the west coast of South America, and learned more about the forces of nature and what they could do. In the Andes, for example, he found beds of fossil shells, marooned at the top of a mountain. Anchored off the coast of Chile, he saw a volcano far in the distance, erupting in the night. It looked, he wrote, like a great star.

Soon after, at Concepción, he witnessed the effects of a devastating earthquake. The quake had destroyed

Top: Darwin observed the
South American ostrich,
or rhea.

Left: The Brazilian rain
forest teems with exotic
life that amazed Darwin.

the town completely; before the Chileans' terrified eyes, it had even altered the shape of the land itself. Before the temblor, they told Darwin, a group of offshore rocks had been below the waterline. And, some miles away, FitzRoy found mussels hanging from rocks well above the high-water mark: another bed of marooned seashells in the making.

As always, Darwin observed, asked questions, made careful notes—and wondered about what he had seen. Meanwhile, the *Beagle* sailed on up the coast to Peru, then changed course for the northwest. It was heading for the equator, and for the Galápagos Islands.

The Galápagos

On September 15, 1835, the *Beagle*, and twenty-six-year-old Charles Darwin, made landfall in the Galápagos archipelago. Although few people lived on this group of volcanic islands, most passing ships stopped there. Here, five hundred miles from the South American mainland, sailors could send and receive mail, refill their water barrels, and stock up with fresh meat. The meat came from the creatures that gave the islands their Spanish name: the *galápagos*, or giant tortoises, that paraded through the island scrub.

Darwin's first reaction to the islands was dismay. The scorching black shore, the parched shrubs and plants, and the spiky cactus did not present an inviting prospect. Soon, however, he changed his mind, as the *Beagle* cruised around the archipelago for a month, stopping at one island after another. Daily, Darwin became more and more fascinated by what he saw. The islands, it seemed, were as rich in mysteries as they were in tortoises.

There was, for instance, the odd behavior of the sea lizards, or iguanas. The sea was their natural habitat—so why did they refuse to enter it when they were frightened? Several times, Darwin hurled a squirming, flailing three-foot reptile into a rock pool. Each time, it swam straight back to shore. Could it be that the iguanas' only enemy were sharks? That might explain why they saw the shoreline's rocks as their best place of safety. It must be a sort of hereditary instinct, handed down from generation to generation.

The birds were fascinating, too. Darwin collected many different types of land birds, half of them finches. Like so much else in the black lands, the male finches were usually black. There were, however, big differences among species. One sort had a massive beak, powerful enough to open tough-shelled seeds. Another had the slender, pointed bill of an insect eater. Others had beaks somewhere in between. And yet they were all finches, living in very similar conditions. Why did they look so different?

Different Islands, Different Tortoises

The tortoises themselves were also creatures of mystery. The first riddle that they presented to Darwin was a small one, easily solved. At first, he could not figure out who, on these desolate islands, made the well worn paths that led from the shore to the hills.

He soon learned that the paths were tortoise trails. For endless generations, the tortoises had walked upon these broad paths up to their regular drinking places, the springs in the middle of the island. Observing this behavior was how the first visitors to the Galápagos had discovered the water there.

The second mystery was not as easy to solve. Darwin was introduced to it by the vice governor of the Galápagos, an Englishman named Nicholas Lawson. Most of the islands had a tortoise population. One day, Lawson casually mentioned that he could tell at a glance which island any captured tortoise had come from. Other islanders said they could do the same. Tortoises from different islands had different markings and different shapes. They

Upon his return from the Galápagos Islands, Darwin realized that he had collected thirteen different finch species.

Right: The sea iguanas of the present-day Galápagos Islands have short, broad heads and strong claws.

Opposite left: Darwin found seagoing iguanas throughout the Galápagos Islands, but the brown land version shown here occurred only on the islands in the middle of the group.

Opposite right: Darwin discovered that each Galápagos island was home to a unique type of tortoise.

even tasted different. The tortoises from James Island, in the middle of the group, were known to be especially delicious.

A Puzzling Question

At first, Darwin did not pay much attention to this local gossip. Then, with a jolt, he realized that he was on the track of something very odd indeed. The islands were very similar. They had similar climates, and most of them were even in sight of each other. Yet each seemed to have its own unique population of creatures.

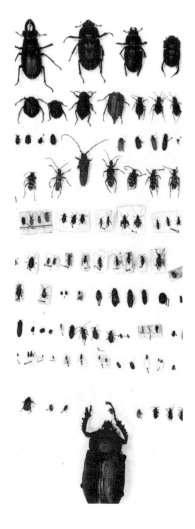

This photograph shows some of the beetles that Darwin collected tirelessly from his earliest years.

Darwin knew the islanders were right—several islands, he was sure, had their own special types of tortoise. Did they also have their own special type of finch? What about the island thrushes, or mockingbirds? It was difficult for Darwin to tell for certain whether each island had its own bird varieties—he had unwittingly mixed up the specimens that he had gathered from the different islands. The perfectionist cursed himself for this error.

How had these differences across species come about, and why? Had all the different tortoises and thrushes really been created by God, each sort for its own little island? Or was there some other explanation? As the *Beagle* sailed away from the islands for good on October 20, 1835, Darwin wrestled with these mysteries.

Hard Work and Recognition

After a voyage that took him over the Pacific, across the Indian Ocean, and northward up through the Atlantic, Charles Darwin, aged twenty-seven, returned home to England in October 1836. To his surprised delight, he found that people had already heard of him and his work.

Other scientists besides Henslow had read the letters Darwin sent back to Cambridge with the carefully packed boxes. Now they wanted to meet him. The great geologist Charles Lyell invited him to dinner. The prestigious Geological Society admitted him to their ranks. Soon he was made the society's secretary. On top of this, he had all his own scientific affairs to see to.

Later, Darwin remembered the two years after his return as the busiest of his life. The *Beagle's* voyage might be over, but his work as its naturalist was scarcely half done. He now had to go through all the specimens he had collected, examine them, classify them, and finally, record the results. Faced with this enormous task, Darwin was nearly paralyzed by despair. With the help of other scientific experts, however, it turned out to be easier than he had expected.

He also had a great deal of writing to do. He edited the five-volume set of books that described the voyage's zoological work. He also wrote a book of his own: his journal of the voyage. It was intended to form a companion volume to two others, written by FitzRoy and by the *Beagle's* earlier captain.

Darwin Rebels

It was impossible for Darwin to carry out all his work from his home in Shrewsbury. So, in 1837, he rented rooms in Great Marlborough Street in central London. He enjoyed all the scientific and social life London had to offer. He soon discovered, however, that he hated the city itself. It was grubby, smelly, and very confining. But he couldn't escape—he had far too much work to do.

After a few months, Darwin rebelled. He felt that his life was becoming as dry and dusty as Great Marlborough Street itself. He had to do something. He could not leave London, so he decided he would create a family life. He began to look for a wife and, the next year, he found one. He did not actually have far to look: she was his first cousin, Emma Wedgwood, the youngest daughter of Uncle Jos. The couple married in 1839 on January 29, shortly before Darwin's thirtieth birthday. That same year, his *Journal of Researches* (of the *Beagle's* voyage) was published.

Health Problems

Emma Darwin came from a big, sociable family, and she soon started to make an inviting and comfortable home for her new husband. People such as Henslow and Lyell were regular visitors. The Darwins also quickly became parents: their first child, William Erasmus Darwin, was born in December 1839.

It soon became clear, however, that something was wrong. As a young man, Darwin had glowed with health and high spirits. He had thrived on the great physical demands of the *Beagle* voyage. Now, however, even though he was back in England and living a much easier life, he frequently felt tired, giddy, and sick. The tiniest effort or excitement left him weak with exhaustion. Simply chatting with

Darwin married Emma Wedgwood in 1839.

friends wore him out. Darwin was famous, he was happily married, he had a growing family, and he had a brilliant future ahead of him. Despite his good fortune, however, he was quickly becoming an invalid—and no one could explain why.

It was obvious to Darwin and Emma that he could not go on with his active life in London. More than anything else, he needed peace and quiet. So, in 1842, the couple left London and moved to the village of Downe in southeast England. Their new home was called Down House. Darwin lived here for the rest of his life, engrossed in his work and seeing few people besides his family and closest friends.

Fear of Controversy?

Over the years, many people have tried to explain what ailed Darwin. One theory is that he had Chagas's disease, an illness carried by the vinchuca bug of South America. Darwin had been bitten by a vinchuca in the Andes.

Other people think that Darwin's problems may have been psychological. He had suffered once already from obvious nerves—in Plymouth, as he impatiently waited for the *Beagle* to set sail, stress had given him a rash and chest pains. Now, he had much more difficult problem to handle—he knew his theories on natural selection could ruin his reputation and career.

By the time of his marriage, Darwin had already started on the work that would one day make him world famous. And he knew, even then, what trouble its publication could cause. People he respected might criticize him, condemn him—even hate him. Darwin, who had always tried to be pleasant to everybody, worried he would not be able to cope with such rejection. And yet, as a scientist, he could not give up trying to understand the implications of his research.

The Evidence of the Birds

Among the specialists who helped Darwin interpret his findings was the London Zoological

A heavy-beaked finch, one of thirteen species on the Galápagos Islands, investigates a cactus in search of food.

Society's ornithologist, John Gould. In 1837, after he had examined the specimens of Galápagos birds that Darwin collected, Gould had determined that they included several different sorts of thrush. And they were not merely different varieties, as Darwin himself had thought. Varieties could breed with each other, to produce hybrids, but the Galápagos thrushes could not have done that. They belonged to three separate species. Gould's report on the finches was even more staggering. Darwin had collected no fewer than thirteen different species.

Because Darwin had mixed the finch specimens together, he could not be sure which islands each one had come from. There was no question, however, where the thrushes had originated. The three different species had come from three different islands, one species to each island. Three species of thrush, thirteen species of finch, and numerous tortoise varieties—it was enough to make Darwin's head spin.

Darwin was certain that the Galápagos creatures must have been blown, carried, or transported in

Left: A seed-eating finch has a large, strong beak.

Right: A warbler finch has a delicate beak because these birds live on insects and fruit.

some other way across the sea from the South American mainland to the islands. He was less sure of what had happened once the animals arrived. Did they start to change—to evolve—into new species? Were there new and different species for each island, for each miniature world cut off from the others by the surrounding sea?

Isolated Islands

Although many of the islands were quite close to each other, a series of strong sea currents streamed through the entire group from east to west. These westerly currents cut off the southern islands from the northern ones. James Island was doubly isolated—between it and the bigger island of Albemarle, another current poured northward.

The islands were further isolated from each other by the winds, or, more accurately, the lack of winds. Darwin remembered the strange, stifling atmosphere of the black lands. No gales blew to carry birds or insects from one island to the next. Once a species somehow got a foothold on one of the Enchanted Isles, Darwin believed, its members stayed there and, over millions of years, began to change. To Darwin, this process made a lot more sense than the idea that God had specially made different creatures for each of these remote specks in the Pacific.

Darwin became obsessed with the challenge of answering the questions raised by his specimens. In July 1837, he set aside a special notebook in which to record anything else he could learn about such changes and variations, anywhere in the world. Charles Darwin had joined the evolutionists.

Lamarck's Giraffe

Evolution was not a completely new idea. Men of science had already begun to question the factual basis of biblical ideas. One of the people who questioned the "creationist" theory was Darwin's own grandfather, Erasmus Darwin, a well-known

....

"It is impossible to reflect on the changed state of the American continent without the deepest astonishment. Formerly it must have swarmed with great monsters: now we find mere pygmies, compared with the antecedent, allied races."

Charles Darwin

....

doctor and thinker. Another was a French naturalist, the Chevalier de Lamarck.

In the early 1800s, Lamarck had declared that all the world's species, humans included, had emerged—or evolved—from other earlier species. The process took place, he argued, because living things all tried to adapt themselves to their living conditions. This, for example, was how giraffes got their long necks. They were descended from hungry, shorter-necked animals who had stretched high into trees for food. A lifetime's stretching, said Lamarck, made these animals' necks grow. And the neck-stretchers' young would also have long necks!

Today, scientists believe that evolution works in the opposite way that Lamarck suggested. The earliest long-necked creatures certainly passed their shape on to their offspring—but they themselves had been born with long necks. Because their necks happened to be longer than average for their species, they could reach into trees for extra food. And, because they could get more food than shorter-necked animals, they tended to live longer. They lived long enough to give birth to long-necked young like themselves.

In its time, however, Lamarck's argument was an intellectual breakthrough. Even though he made a mistake about how evolution works, by boldly stating that evolution itself took place, he provoked other scientists to think and argue about it. Lamarck's views were bitterly opposed by the leading French naturalist of the day, Baron Georges Cuvier, a creationist.

Darwin Begins Work

It was at this point in the debate that Darwin began his major work. He intended for his research to be simple. At first, he rejected the goal of trying to prove or disprove a preconceived theory. Instead, he planned to do the opposite—collect facts about the differences among living things. He would use any and all facts, as many as he possibly could find,

Darwin made this detailed drawing of a beetle. He took painstaking care while he recorded his findings.

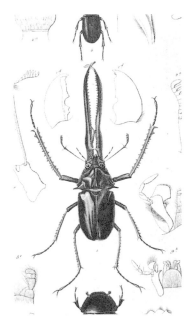

While at work on his theory of evolution, Darwin took up pigeon-keeping.

drawn from as many sources as he could contact. Only when he had finished collecting facts would he try to determine what they all meant.

In this way, Darwin started his great project. When he could spare time from his *Beagle* work, he talked to animal breeders and gardeners. He sent off questionnaires to scientists. He read enormously. At Down House, he observed and experimented tirelessly: watching his collection of pigeons, studying the pollination of the Down holly trees, and cross-breeding cabbage varieties and analyzing the results.

In 1838, Darwin happened to read a book by an influential British economist, Thomas Malthus, that shed new light on his work. Called *An Essay on the Principle of Population*, the book painted a grim future for the human race. Malthus calculated that, left completely to their own devices, human populations increased very quickly. They doubled every twenty-five years. Food supplies could never increase so fast, so humans were constantly threatened by starvation. The only things that kept populations under control were disasters like war, famine, and disease. If some people were to live, others had to die. Existence itself was a constant struggle.

The phrase "every twenty-five years" echoed through Darwin's brain. Malthus was referring to humans, but Darwin wondered about animals and plants. They sometimes doubled their populations in days rather than years. All of them were faced with a savage competition for what nourishment was available. There was not—there never could be—enough food to feed every living thing on earth. Many living things perished: that is what Darwin had observed in the past. Other living things survived.

And who were these survivors? They were the creatures and plants that were best suited to their circumstances. They were the ones who were just a little different from the rest—the ones who were better equipped to win the competition. And, winning it, they survived to breed; so would their offspring, and their offspring's offspring.

Darwin's Theory

It was a long time before Darwin was able to propose his theory of evolution in its final form. Only two years after returning to Britain, however, he had already worked out its central idea. The theory's basic message was simple. Evolution, it said, did take place. The world's species had not been shaped in one single burst of divine creation. Instead, they had developed—evolved—from species that had existed earlier.

The force that made new species evolve, Darwin said, was "natural selection"—the process that ensured the preservation of physical features that helped an individual to survive. Within a species, these special features were handed down from one generation of survivors to another. In the end, they were shared by a huge number of individuals. These

This painting depicts the biblical story of the survival of species. As the great flood threatens the world, Noah loads breeding pairs of the world's creatures into the ark. Anything that did not enter the ark became extinct as soon as the flood covered the earth.

41

individuals would now all be members of a new species—a different species from which they had originated.

One or more even newer species could spring from these new species. They, in turn, could parent many more. And, as time went by, the newcomer species would vary more and more widely, both from each other and from their original parent species.

"Confessing a Murder"

Darwin spent about fourteen years at work on his theory. He tested it, thought of potential objections to it, and formulated answers to those objections. In 1842, he jotted down a rough outline in pencil of his views. He wrote a longer version in 1844, when he was thirty-five. Around this time, he told a friend that he thought species did change over time; making this statement was, he said, "like confessing a murder."

Darwin took such trouble with his research because he knew there was only one way to gain acceptance for such radical ideas. Each step in his argument had to be backed up with hard, solid evidence—evidence that even the most fervent of creationists could not deny.

A Contented Life

Soon after Darwin's so-called confession, he took a break—an eight-year break—from evolution, and studied barnacles instead. He emerged from this work as a fully trained biologist, which helped enormously when he returned to his species projects.

His health, though, did not allow him to work more than a few hours a day. The rest of the time he read, walked, wrote innumerable letters, and played backgammon with Emma. (He always kept score, and his records show that he was a better player than his wife—but just barely.)

His routine seldom changed. He would arise early and take a stroll in the garden no matter what the weather. He ate breakfast at 7:45, then went straight into his study to work until 9:30: the best working time of the day, he always said. Then, the mail arrived; he took a break until 10:30, and worked again until about noon. Noon marked the end of his working day; feeling satisfied, Darwin would call to one of his beloved dogs and take another walk.

His route usually led him to the little wood he and Emma had created in a far corner of the grounds. In it were big old oaks that had been growing there for hundreds of years. To this, he had added lime trees, hazels, and hollies, while Emma had planted flowering shrubs. All around it ran a path, covered with sand dug from a pit within the wood itself. The family called it the "Sand-walk." Darwin loved it, and his children—who now numbered four—made it their special playground.

He adored his children and they adored him in return. He spent a lot of time with them. When they were ill, he would turn his study into a sickroom: the patient would curl up on a sofa while the great scientist worked alongside. When the children were healthy, he let them help with his research; they performed tasks such as following bees around the

Emma Darwin, shown here sitting in a window of Down House, frequently read aloud to her children.

When the nonnative squirrel (left) was introduced into Britain, it began to compete with the native red squirrel (right) for food and living space. Since the nonnative squirrel is bigger and can eat a more varied diet than the red squirrel, it is now more common. This process illustrates Darwin's idea that the struggle for survival is much more severe when it occurs between closely related species.

garden to plot the insects' regular routes. All the same, the children thought their father worked too hard: one of them, at the age of four, once even tried to bribe him to come out and play.

Darwin's days were a placid mixture of methodical work and happy, comfortable family life. He had plenty of money, inherited from his father. He did not need to earn any. There was no reason for him to do anything he did not want to do—and that included publishing his species theory, his life's work, to be judged, criticized, and probably attacked.

Tragedy and Support

In 1858, Alfred Russel Wallace's letter from the East Indies came crashing into Darwin's peaceful life. The letter could not have come at a worse time. While Darwin agonized over what to do, scarlet fever—an often fatal disease in those days—had appeared in the village. Within days, it reached the nursery at Down House. A few days later, it killed the Darwins' youngest son, Charles Waring Darwin.

For a short while, the scientist was crushed by the two misfortunes that had befallen him. He was supported, however, by devoted friends that included Charles Lyell and Sir Joseph Hooker, assistant director of the Royal Botanic Gardens at Kew. Lyell and Hooker calmed Darwin's anxiety, convinced him not to allow Wallace to announce his findings first, and arranged for the joint Darwin-Wallace reading to the Linnean Society of London. The scientists who heard the reading received it with interest, but they were cautious in both their praise and their criticism. They did not want to antagonize the powerful Lyell and Hooker.

Darwin himself was relieved that the reading had not generated the controversy he had expected. He now agreed with his friends that he must publish something on his theory as soon as possible. During a visit to the Isle of Wight, he started writing his book *The Origin of Species*, which began, "When on board HMS *Beagle*, as naturalist, I was much struck with certain facts."

A Subtle Statement

By Darwin's own standards—and by those of the nineteenth century—*The Origin of Species* was a fairly short book. Even so, it presented more than six hundred pages of argument and evidence. On the third-to-last page appeared one of the most important sentences of all. Acceptance of his views, Darwin said, would cause a revolution in the study of natural history. New fields of research would be opened up. And "much light will be thrown on the origin of man and his history."

This statement is one of the few about the human race that appear in the book. And it is clear what Darwin was trying to do. He had his own definite views on the origin of the human species, and they were even more controversial than his other ideas. With that one sentence, Darwin suggested that he had not yet worked out how humans fitted into his theory.

If Darwin thought this statement would placate creationists, he was fooling himself. Only five pages earlier, he had written, "I believe that animals are

Writing in the 1850s, Darwin observed that "cats which are entirely white and have blue eyes are generally deaf."

descended from at most only four or five progenitors, and plants from an equal or lesser number." This declaration was followed, more tentatively, by the suggestion that all plants and animals might be descended from one single ancestral form. And what, from any rational point of view, were humans, if not animals?

Under its full title—*On the Origin of Species by Means of Natural Selection, or the Preservation of Favoured Races in the Struggle for Life*—Charles Darwin's book was published in London on November 24, 1859. The publisher, John Murray, printed 1,250 copies. Darwin worried that Murray would be left with unsold stock, but he was wrong. Before the day was out, British booksellers had placed an order for every copy.

A Monkey for a Grandmother?

The publication of the book soon created the kind of outcry that Darwin had always anticipated. In 1860, at a meeting of the British Association for the Advancement of Science held at the Oxford University Museum of Natural History, the controversy reached a pinnacle. There, Thomas Henry Huxley, a leading biologist and Darwin supporter, squared off with clergyman Samuel Wilberforce, Bishop of Oxford, in a debate over Darwin's book.

Wilberforce himself did not understand all of the intricacies of Darwin's theories. An assistant had briefed him, and the clergyman, well known for his stirring oratory, delivered an impassioned speech that held the audience in spellbound silence. At the speech's end, in the hot, breathless quiet of the room, one sentence seemed to hang in the air like an echo. Its words were courteous, formal, even witty—but they dripped with venom. Was it, the bishop had asked the scientist, on his grandfather's side or his grandmother's that he was descended from a monkey?

After a stunned moment, the audience—most of whom agreed with Wilberforce—applauded wildly

"Can we doubt (remembering that many more individuals are born than can possibly survive) that individuals having any advantage, however slight, over others, would have the best chance of surviving and of procreating their kinds? On the other hand, we may feel sure that any variation in the least degree injurious would be rigidly destroyed."

Charles Darwin, from *The Origin of Species*

as the bishop sat down. Wilberforce looked around happily. His speech had gone very well, and would no doubt put an end to this heretical theory of Mr. Darwin's. Wilberforce did not notice when, with an air of triumph, his opponent slapped himself on the knee. Huxley had just thought of the right reply.

A Retort for the Bishop

From all around the hall came calls for Professor Huxley to speak. Professor Henslow, in the chair, nodded to his fellow scientist, and Huxley stood up.

Huxley, unlike Wilberforce, was a quiet, plain speaker, and his speech began quietly. He defended Darwin; he explained what Darwin's theory meant; he cast doubts on the bishop's grasp of science. And then, abruptly, he closed in for the kill.

Suppose that the bishop was right, he said. Suppose that he—Huxley—was descended from a

Middle-class Victorian women were expected to act as the "angel in the house," the protector of morals, and the source of everything beautiful in domestic life. This cartoon of the 1860s expresses the view that such a being could not possibly be related to wild, hairy apes.

monkey. What of it? He would rather be descended from an ape, he declared firmly, than from a man who "used great gifts to obscure the truth." Or, in other words, from such a cultured, honey-tongued spreader of mischief and error as the bishop himself.

Instantly, there was pandemonium. There were cheers, boos, shrieks of laughter, and tumultuous clapping. Seated near Huxley on the speakers' platform, Darwin's friend Joseph Hooker relaxed. The bishop sat silent and mortified. A group of other clergymen protested furiously. Further back in the hall, Oxford students whooped and yelled with delight. Near the windows, a fashionable lady fainted with shock.

Samuel Wilberforce, the Bishop of Oxford, vehemently rejected Darwin's theory.

"During the voyage of the *Beagle* I had been deeply impressed by discovering . . . great fossil animals covered with armour like that on the existing armadillos; secondly, by the manner in which closely allied animals replace one another in proceeding southwards over the Continent. . . . It was evident that such facts as these, as well as many others, could only be explained on the supposition that species gradually became modified; and the subject haunted me. But it was equally evident that neither the action of the surrounding conditions, nor the will of the organisms (especially in the case of plants) could account for the innumerable cases in which organisms of every kind are beautifully adapted to their habits of life."

Charles Darwin, on how he started his work on *The Origin of Species*

Perhaps most outrageous, in the thick of the audience, a man had leaped to his feet, yelling and holding high a Bible. Here, he shouted, was the source of all truth: here and here alone. He was the *Beagle*'s old captain, Robert FitzRoy—by now fifty-four, a vice-admiral, a religious zealot, and an ardent creationist.

"Darwin's Bulldog"

By the end of the meeting, it was plain that Darwin's side had won, even though Darwin himself was absent due to illness. In people like Huxley and Hooker, Darwin had found champions who could defend him much better than he could ever defend himself.

Huxley was, in fact, a new arrival in the Darwin camp. He had been asked to review *The Origin of Species* for Britain's leading newspaper, the *Times*, and he had praised it warmly. This was a great piece of luck for both Darwin and his theory. From then on, Huxley sprang to Darwin's defense whenever necessary and was soon known as "Darwin's bulldog."

As the Oxford meeting showed, the "bulldog" was a valuable ally. Darwinism—as it was called—had some formidable enemies. Most were religious opponents, but some scientists disagreed with the theory as well.

The scientists' group attacked Darwin on several different grounds. One complaint focused on Darwin's working methods. All he had done, critics said, was prove what he wanted to prove, a notoriously easy task. Others objected to the time period in which, according to Darwin, evolution had taken place. No scientist believed that the world was only four thousand years old, but 300 million years, Darwin's figure, seemed too big a leap in the other direction. (Most scientists today believe even Darwin's guess was a colossal underestimation.)

Other scientists questioned how heredity worked. Just how did the fastest, strongest, or most adaptable

Biologist Thomas Henry Huxley defended Darwin's theory so energetically that he became known as "Darwin's bulldog."

creatures pass their special gifts on to their offspring? No one at the time, Darwin included, could guess that the answers to this question were already emerging—and they would support Darwin's theory. In a monastery garden in central Europe, a Czech named Gregor Mendel was crossbreeding varieties of garden peas and studying the results. His work eventually formed the basis of the modern science of genetics.

A Threat to Authority

Unlike the scientific objections, the religious ones tended to cluster around one issue. Everyone saw through Darwin's attempt to keep humans out of his theory. It was obvious that, if his law of natural selection worked, it worked for humans as well.

This meant that humans were not made in God's image. They were not the lords of creation, the superiors of everything else in the world. They were living creatures like any other, and had evolved from earlier living creatures.

Arguments like these directly threatened the Christian church's authority. Until then, Christians had believed what the Bible told them. If the Bible was proved wrong, what did that do to their most sacred beliefs?

Darwin's critics said he was linking the human race with monkeys—smelly, hairy creatures famous for their pranks and wild behavior. In fact, Darwin never suggested that humans were descended from the great apes. Nonetheless, the idea was perpetuated by Darwin's enemies. People made monkey jokes and sang monkey songs. Magazines printed monkey cartoons.

Darwinism Meets a Need

The Darwinists faced formidable opposition—the combined might of the church and most of the scientific world. Even more discouraging was the fact that many people seemed to have misunderstood Darwin's theory. Darwin's supporters never managed to erase all the religious opposition. With their fellow

Even though Darwin never suggested that humans were descended from great apes, the idea was attributed to him and widely mocked in cartoons, songs, and jokes.

51

This artist's rendering shows an archaeopteryx, which scientists believe had scales, a long tail, and teeth like a reptile, along with feathers like a bird.

scientists, however, they had far more success—and this victory came surprisingly fast.

Darwin's theory met a need that biologists were only beginning to realize they had. They lacked a scientific method of thinking about the origin of species—one that dealt in facts, measurements, and proofs. Before Darwin, all they had was a religious method of thinking—a method that dealt in beliefs, feelings, and statements that could not be proved. Evolution, as explained by Darwin, gave scientists a truly scientific way of thinking.

The Theory Gains Support

Few scientists agreed with all of Darwin's theory. The idea of natural selection, in particular, troubled them. Their reservations were assuaged partly, however, because Darwin did not say that natural selection was the only force that powered evolution—just the main one. Darwinism also got a boost when, in 1861, fossils were discovered in Germany that proved the theory on one point: the evolutionary link between reptiles and birds. The German fossils were the remains of an archaeopteryx. It had a reptile's bones, a reptile's tail, and feathers.

Darwin's theory was bolstered most of all by Huxley and his helpers. Darwin's "bulldog" and his colleagues were influential men—and, as Darwinism became more widely accepted, they became more influential still. Not surprisingly, they used their influence to make sure that university jobs went to young, promising Darwinists.

By 1870, nearly 75% of Britain's biologists had become evolutionists. In the 1880s, scientists who did not support Darwin's views were the exception rather than the rule. Darwinism took root in the United States as well, and in parts of Europe. In Japan—then just emerging from a feudal past of shoguns and samurai—modern thinkers read translations of Darwin's theory and agreed with it.

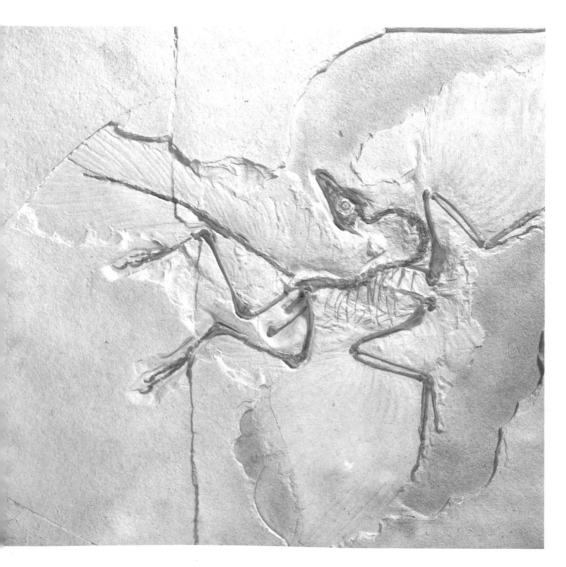

The unbelievable had happened. Charles Darwin had won.

Fossil evidence of the archaeopteryx supported Darwin's theory.

Darwin's Work Continues

Darwin was now in his fifties, and his daily life continued just as before. The scientists argued, the churchmen inveighed, and the energetic Huxley fought battles openly and behind the scenes. Through it all, at Down House, the scientist who had started all the controversy went on with his normal routine of work, walks, rests, and listening to Emma play the piano.

Although Darwin's working hours were short, he accomplished a great deal. First, he revised *The Origin of Species*. It went into six separate editions; in his usual painstaking way, Darwin continually altered and corrected them. He compiled additional findings into book form or wrote them up in scientific papers. Darwin also wrote a stream of articles for magazines, on subjects that ranged from chemistry to hedgehogs.

Evolution and natural selection were threads that linked most of Darwin's work. The book that followed *The Origin of Species*, for instance, looked at the effect evolution had had on the way orchids were pollinated. A paper on climbing plants showed how their tendrils helped their chances of survival.

The Origins of the Human Species

Eventually, Darwin tackled the most daunting subject of all—the one he had skirted in *The Origin of Species*. In 1867, at age fifty-eight, he started writing a book on the origins of the human species.

The result, called *The Descent of Man*, was published in 1871. In it, Darwin plunged boldly into describing the links—the taboo links—that bound human beings to the animal world, and especially to the apes.

Darwin pointed out that humans and apes have similar bodies and sense organs. They catch some of the same diseases. The human embryo and the ape embryo develop in similar ways: both, for a while, have tails, but this vestige of a four-footed ancestor vanishes by the time they are born. The similarities do not stop there. Humans and animals experience similar emotions, such as happiness and boredom. And the human race's greatest asset, intelligence, is also, to a lesser extent, found in animals.

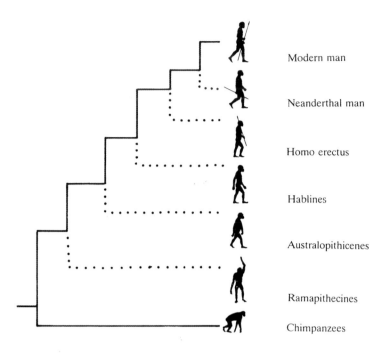

Modern man

Neanderthal man

Homo erectus

Hablines

Australopithicenes

Ramapithecines

Chimpanzees

None of this, Darwin said, meant that humans were actually descended from apes. What it did mean was that, way back in the distant past, humans and apes had evolved from the same ancestral species: a four-footed one, at that.

Here at last, backed with a mass of convincing detail, was the notorious Charles Darwin's answer to the story of Adam and Eve. As Darwin expected, the book caused a sensation. The church deplored it, reviewers attacked it, and the book-reading public rushed to buy it.

Among scientists, the climate of opinion was changing fast, in support of Darwinism. The idea that evolution applied to all living things had become easier and easier to accept. Huxley himself, in 1863, had published a book called *Evidence of Man's Place in Nature*. In many ways, the battle over humanity's origins had been fought and won

This diagram shows Darwin's view that humans are not descended from apes but do share a common ancestor.

This famous painting depicts Emma Darwin, who was a gifted pianist, playing for her husband.

before Darwin started to write his own book on the subject.

The Final Years

Darwin spent the last ten years of his life much as he had spent the thirty years before: he stayed mainly at Down House, worked, and enjoyed the company of his family and much-loved pets. His troubled health began to improve. He did not seem to be ill any more—just tired. His life's work was completed. The subject that had haunted him for so long had, at last, been defined, put into words, and launched upon the world. It could go its own way now. And he could go on to new pursuits: studying the movement of earthworms and writing his autobiography.

At the end of 1881, Darwin suffered a heart attack. He recovered, but the following spring, when he was seventy-three years old, he had another, and then a third. On the afternoon of April 19, 1882, Charles Darwin died.

At first, Emma and his children wanted him to be buried at the local village church. The public, however—Parliament, scientists, and journalists—thought otherwise, and the family relented. On April 26, 1882, as a mark of the deepest national respect, the reluctant enemy of the Church was buried in Westminster Abbey in London.

Discoveries in Many Fields

Scientists use a phrase called "evolutionary synthesis." The name was made famous in a book by Sir Julian Huxley, the grandson of Darwin's old friend. "Synthesis" means "bringing together," and evolutionary synthesis is based on the findings of many scientists who worked in many different fields, all of whom found their research to be consistent with Darwin's theories.

The first of these scientists was the monk Gregor Mendel, who had read Darwin's work. Mendel's discoveries in genetics were ignored for many years, then rediscovered in 1900. Mendel discovered the patterns by which living creatures pass on their features from one generation to the next. Mendel observed, for example, that if tall peas were crossbred with dwarf ones, all the hybrids were tall. If two of these tall hybrids were then crossed, a quarter of their offspring would be dwarf. Mendel worked out why this happened, but he could not explain what, exactly, the plants were handing on to each other: what shape that "factor" for tallness or dwarfness took.

The White-Eyed Flies

The scientists who studied Mendel's work included an American zoologist, Thomas Hunt Morgan. Working with fast-breeding fruit flies, he began to study mutations: suddenly occurring differences in

"No fact in the long history of the world is so startling as the wide and repeated exterminations of its inhabitants."

Charles Darwin

57

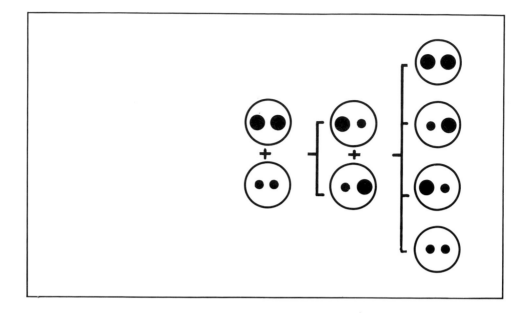

This diagram, based on the work of Gregor Mendel, shows how living things inherit traits from each of their parents.

individual members of a species. In 1910, he found he could breed a new strain of flies with white eyes. He also found that all the white-eyed flies were male; thus, the "white-eye factor" was linked to its owner's sex.

Morgan went on to identify the "factor" itself, which he now called a gene. He could say where in the flies' bodies it was: he found that these basic building blocks of heredity lay on the threadlike chromosomes present in the flies' body cells. Morgan's discovery was a big step forward, even though the workings of genes still remained a mystery.

Genes and DNA

Scientists continued to learn more about chromosomes, genes, and the mathematics of natural selection. As more and more details emerged of how life functioned, people realized that Darwin's findings and Mendel's fitted together.

Julian Huxley's book about evolutionary synthesis appeared in 1942. It was soon followed by further key developments. Scientists studying DNA, a chemical found in chromosomes, discovered that DNA was the "messenger" they were looking for. It was the substance that was transmitted from one generation to the next, one that passed on the instructions of heredity. DNA was, in fact, made of genes.

In the 1960s, the genetic code—the chemical code in which heredity's instructions are expressed—began to be cracked. Further, researchers discovered that this code was the same for all living creatures. Darwin's tentative conclusion that all organisms were "descended from some one prototype" had received the most unexpected backing.

The Ideas Live On

Every step in the discovery of how life works throws new light on the theory of evolution. Even today, however, scientists insist that it remains a theory: the time periods involved are too big to allow for final, irrefutable proof.

For this reason, controversy over Darwinism continues. In the scientific world, new ideas about evolution are constantly proposed. Meanwhile, some people still oppose evolution on religious grounds. Frequently, in school districts where evolution is taught in science classes, parents and community leaders insist that creationism be given equal time.

There are also a number of people, scientists and Christians alike, who believe that Darwinism and creationism are not necessarily mutually exclusive. They use the same argument that Galileo Galilei used, two hundred years before *The Origin of Species* was published, to defend his then-heretical theory that the earth was not the center of the universe. This argument states that if God created the

> "Charles Darwin is the father of modern biology. His ideas remain at the heart of it."
>
> Colin Tudge, speaking on BBC Radio, July 30, 1989

> "Some check is constantly preventing the too-rapid increase of every organised being left in a state of nature. The supply of food, on average, remains constant; yet the tendency in every animal to increase by propagation is geometrical. . . . In a species long established, any great increase in numbers is obviously impossible, and must be checked by some means."
>
> Charles Darwin

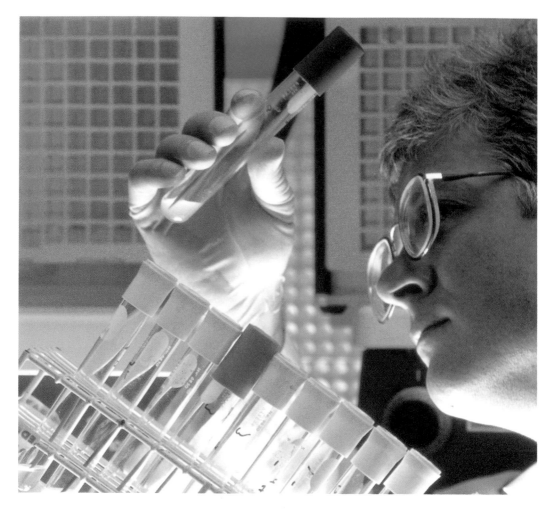

Scientists today continue to unlock the mysteries of genetics.

universe—as Christianity teaches—then he also created physical laws, such as gravity and time, that govern it. Therefore, if evolution is another process that governs the universe, evolution was created by God. One clergyman who holds this view says, "Evolution is simply a scientific understanding of our origins. It does not make God unnecessary."

Darwin himself realized 150 years ago that controversy and his theory are tightly bound together. The fact that people still argue over Darwinism is proof of its importance. Darwin's legacy to science has changed over the years, but the ideas he worked out so painstakingly still resound, both in scientific circles and elsewhere.

Timeline

1809   Charles Robert Darwin is born in Shrewsbury, England.

1818   Darwin goes to Shrewsbury School as a boarder.

1825   Darwin goes to Edinburgh University to study medicine.

1826   Darwin reads his first scientific paper to the university natural-history society.

1828   Charles Darwin enrolls in Cambridge University.

1831   Darwin meets Captain FitzRoy and is accepted for the post of naturalist on the HMS *Beagle*. The *Beagle* sets sail for South America.

1832–34   The *Beagle* sails up and down the eastern coast of South America. The main destinations include Salvador, Rio de Janeiro, Montevideo, and the Tierra del Fuego region. Darwin discovers fossilized giants at Punta Alta, Argentina, in 1833.

1834   The *Beagle* enters the Pacific.

1835   After voyaging up the west coast of South America, the *Beagle* reaches the Galápagos Archipelago.

1835–36   The *Beagle* makes her homeward voyage via New Zealand, Australia, the Indian Ocean, and the Cape of Good Hope. The ship arrives in England on October 2, 1836.

1837   In London, Darwin begins to study the evolution of species.

1838   Darwin reads Malthus's *Population*, and sees the connection between evolution and the struggle of all species for survival.

1839   Charles Darwin marries his cousin, Emma Wedgwood. His journal of the *Beagle's* voyage is published.

1842   Darwin starts writing a pencil sketch of his species theory. The Darwins move to Down House.

1844   Darwin writes a longer version of his species theory.

1846   Darwin starts his eight-year study of barnacles.

1856   Darwin begins to write his "big book," in which he outlines his theory of evolution by natural selection.

1858   Darwin receives Wallace's letter. Both his early sketch of his theory and Wallace's paper are read to the Linnean Society. Darwin starts work on *The Origin of Species*.

1859   *The Origin of Species* is published in London.

1860	Professor T.H. Huxley, "Darwin's bulldog," debates Bishop Samuel Wilberforce at the annual meeting of the British Association for the Advancement of Science.
1862	Darwin publishes a book on orchid pollination.
1864	The Copley Medal of the Royal Society is awarded to Darwin for his work on geology, zoology, and botany.
1868	Darwin publishes his *Variation of Animals and Plants under Domestication*.
1871	*The Descent of Man* is published.
1872	Darwin publishes his *Expression of the Emotions in Man and Animals*.
1881	Darwin publishes his last book, *The Formation of Vegetable Mould, Through the Action of Worms*. While visiting a friend in London, he has a heart attack.
1882	Charles Darwin dies at Down at the age of seventy-three and is buried at Westminster Abbey in London.

Glossary

Archaeopteryx: The earliest form of bird yet discovered, with features of both birds and reptiles.

Archipelago: The technical name for a group of islands.

Biology: The study of living things.

Botany: The scientific study of plant life.

Capybara: The world's largest living rodent, native to South America.

Cell: A minute block of jelly-like substance, enclosed in a membrane. It is the basic unit out of which all living organisms are made.

Chromosomes: The threadlike structures found within the nucleus of a cell.

Creationism: The belief that all the world's species were made by God during the six-day period of Creation described in the Christian Bible, and that the forms in which they were made have never changed.

Darwinism: The theory that new species evolve through natural selection.

DNA: The abbreviation for deoxyribonucleic acid, the chemical found inside chromosomes that carries the genetic instructions for the way cells should develop.

Evolution: The process by which something gradually develops into something different and new.

Factor (of heredity): The earlier name for gene.

Fossil: The buried remains of once-living creatures preserved in some form by the action of the earth.

Genes: The chemical instructions, carried on the DNA in the chromosomes, by which parents pass on their characteristics to their young.

Geology: The study of earth formations.

Heredity: The passing on of characteristics from parents to offspring.

Hybrid: The offspring produced by breeding different varieties of animals or plants.

Natural history: The name that, in Darwin's time, was given to the scientific study of plants and animals.

Natural selection: The process by which individual organisms that are specially well-equipped to exploit their surroundings hand on their special characteristics to increasing numbers of descendants, finally giving rise to a new species in which all members share the original special feature.

Ornithology: The scientific study of birds.

Species: A group of organisms that are alike, and that can produce offspring that are themselves capable of producing offspring.

Variety: A group of distinctive—and closely similar—organisms within a single species.

Zoology: The scientific study of animal life.

For More Information

Books

Barter, James. *The Galápagos Islands*. San Diego: Lucent Books, 2002.

Burton, Jane. *The Nature and Science of Survival*. Milwaukee, WI: Gareth Stevens, 2001.

Darwin, Charles. *The Origin of Species*. Ed. Greg Suriano. New York: Grammercy, 1998.

Fullick, Ann. *Charles Darwin*. Portsmouth, NH: Heinemann, 2000.

Nardo, Don. *Charles Darwin*. San Diego: Greenhaven Press, 2000.

———. *The Origin of Species: Darwin's Theory of Evolution*. San Diego: Lucent Books, 2001.

Sonder, Ben. *Evolution and Creationism*. Danbury, CT: Franklin Watts, 1999.

Stefoff, Rebecca. *Charles Darwin and the Evolution Revolution*. New York: Oxford University Press, 1998.

Websites

Charles Darwin: The Origin of the Species and The Voyage of the Beagle
www.literature.org/authors/darwin-charles

Charles Darwin, British Naturalist
www2.lucidcafe.com/lucidcafe/library/96feb/darwin.html

Evolution and Natural Selection
www.sprl.umich.edu/GCL/paper_to_html/selection.html#DARWIN

The Galápagos Islands
www.encyclopedia.com/articles/04858.html

Index